THE BUSY MAN'S
GUIDE
TO REKINDLING THE GLOW

— 50 Suggestions To Rekindle The Glow

Sue Landis

Writers Club Press

San Jose • New York • Lincoln • Shanghai

The Busy Man's Guide To Rekindling The Glow:
50 Suggestions To Rekindle The Glow

Published by Writers Club Press
an imprint of iUniverse.com, Inc.

For information address:
iUniverse.com, Inc.
620 North 48th Street
Suite 201
Lincoln, NE 68504-3467
www.iuniverse.com

ISBN: 0-595-09759-6

Printed in the United States of America

To all you wonderful men who know and feel these things, but sometimes forget to show and tell that special woman in your life.

CONTENTS

ACKNOWLEDGEMENTS

A warm thank you to my friends, you encouraged me by reading this book and making suggestions or just plain enjoying it. You are in my heart center.

All the quotations were taken from Microsoft Bookshelf 1987-1995 version, which used The Columbia Dictionary of Quotations.

INTRODUCTION

Dear Wonderful Man:

When "life happens," the passions in our main relationship sometimes take second, third, fourth or last place. Without noticing, we lay aside our physical playfulness.

To use this book, go to any page. Each page has a single suggestion, endearing statement, quote or trick to the trade. Try what may appeal to you or your lady, allowing for variety.

Be playful. Be patient. Reap the rewards.

Gentlemen, plan your play. Play your plan.

Sue Landis

SUGGESTION 1

Phone your lady on the way to work.

If she is out, leave this message. "Hi. I was thinking warm thoughts about you and wanted to let you know I love you."

This is a love message only so get off the phone. If you call from your cell phone in the car, make sure you stop, letting her know you are giving her your undivided attention.

Endearing Statement

"I like
the scent
of your body."

Quote

A man falls in love through his eyes, a woman through her ears.

Woodrow Wyatt (b. 1918), British journalist. To the Point, "The Ears Have It" (1981)

SUGGESTION 2

Hug your lady.

Embrace her for at least 10 seconds.

Be silent. Let your warm embrace be your words. Let her know that it is safe to come to you for touching when she is not feeling sexual, like when she is feeling blue or happy for no apparent reason.

Endearing Statement

"I like
the softness
of your skin."

Quote

Sex is like money; only too much is enough.

John Updike (b. 1932), U.S. author, critic. Piet Hanema, in Couples, ch. 5 (1968).

SUGGESTION 3

Come up behind your lady.

Place your hands on her shoulders and very lightly slide your hands down her arms, allowing your fingers to ever so gently glide between the spaces of her fingers.

Do it again, making a purring sound.

Allow her to savor your caresses, your purring, and your smile.

Endearing Statement

"I feel
toasty warm
when next
to you."

Quote

Love is an act of endless forgiveness, a tender look which becomes a habit.

Peter Ustinov (b. 1921), British actor, writer, director. *Christian Science Monitor* (Boston, 9 Dec. 1958).

SUGGESTION 4

During the day, as you pass your lady, allow your hand to gently caress one of her buttocks.

Softly say, "Nice. Very nice."

Walk away, with an admiring backward glance. Your lady likes to be admired.

Allow her the space to conclude that you still find HER desirable.

Taking your time with her will enhance the rewards.

Endearing Statement

"I like
looking at
your face."

Quote

Sex appeal is fifty percent what you've got and fifty percent what people think you've got.

Sophia Loren (b. 1934), Italian actor. Quoted in: Leslie Halliwell, *Halliwell's Filmgoer's Companion* (1984).

SUGGESTION 5

Be a poet. Write a poem.

You do not have to be good or even rhyme.

Tell your lady she is the sunshine in your life.

Give her warm sensations and she will feel good about herself and about you.

Avoid crudeness to achieve romance.

Endearing Statement

"I like to look
at the curves of
your breasts.
They are
beautiful."

Quote

Falling in love consists merely in uncorking the imagination and bottling the common-sense.

Helen Rowland (1875–1950), U.S. journalist. *A Guide to Men,* "Variations" (1922).

SUGGESTION 6

Use the next four suggestions on separate days in order to heighten the anticipation for both of you.

Surprise your lady by putting a single, long stem, red rose on her pillow, so she finds it when she prepares for bed.

Remove the thorns. Have a vase handy.

Let her make advances if she so chooses.

Play to the mystery.

Endearing Statement

"I like
the curves
of your arms."

Quote

What angel wakes me from my flow'ry bed?

William Shakespeare (1564–1616), English dramatist, poet. Titania, woken by Bottom's singing, in *A Midsummer Night's Dream,* act 3, sc. 1.

SUGGESTION 7

The day after placing the rose on her pillow, phone your lady.

Tell her you want to take that delicate, velvety, red rose and gently rub it on her skin until she has the scent of roses.

Tell her you want to start by caressing her neck, trailing the petals between her breasts, curving around each beautiful breast.

Play to the drama.

Endearing Statement

"Your kisses
delight me."

Quote

Love is the final end of the world's history, the Amen of the universe.

Novalis [Friedrich von Hardenberg] (1772–1801), German poet, novelist. *Thoughts on Religion,* pt. 1 in *Hymns and Thoughts on Religion* (tr. and ed. by W. Hastie, 1888), from *Fragments* (1799–1800).

SUGGESTION 8

The day after telling your lady you would like to make love to her with a rose, call her in the morning from your office.

Ask her to go to the store and get a fresh, pert rose so you can caress her lovely body that evening.

Play the drama of expectation and anticipation.

Endearing Statement

"I like
when you giggle."

Quote

If there hadn't been women we'd still be squatting in a cave eating raw meat, because we made civilization in order to impress our girl friends. And they tolerated it and let us go ahead and play with our toys.

Orson Welles (1915–85), U.S. filmmaker, actor, producer. Interview in David Frost, *The Americans,* "Can a Martian Survive by Pretending to be a Leading American Actor?" (1970).

SUGGESTION 9

Ask your lady to caress your body with a rose.

Tell her you want to know how she felt.

Endearing Statement

"I like
to hear you sing
when you think
no one is around."

Quote

We've got this gift of love, but love is like a precious plant. You can't just accept it and leave it in the cupboard or just think it's going to get on by itself. You've got to keep watering it. You've got to really look after it and nurture it.

John Lennon (1940–80), British rock musician. *Man of the Decade,* broadcast, 30 Dec. 1969, ATV.

SUGGESTION 10

Whisper in your lady's ear that you want to buy massage oil for her.

Ask her if she has a favorite scent.

Even better, ask her to meet you at the store.

Endearing Statement

"I like
watching you
when you are reading."

Quote

Do you want me to tell you something really subversive?
Love is everything it's cracked up to be. That's why
people are so cynical about it.... It really is worth fighting
for, being brave for, risking everything for. And the
trouble is, if you don't risk anything, you risk even more.

Erica Jong (b. 1942), U.S. author. Hans, in *How to Save
Your Own Life,* "Intuition, extuition..." (1977).

SUGGESTION 11

Give your lady a full body massage without initiating sex.

Take your time. Explore her body, as if, this were the first time.

Make sounds, letting her know you receive pleasure from touching her.

Go slowly for maximum benefits.

Endearing Statement

"I like
holding your hand."

Quote

How beautiful maleness is, if it finds its right expression.

D. H. Lawrence (1885–1930), British author. *Sea and Sardinia,* ch. 3 (1923).

SUGGESTION 12

Before you fall asleep, hold your lady's hand or put your arm around her and draw her close.

Tell her you enjoy her natural body scent and feel of her skin.

Tell her, it is a pleasure touching her.

Let her initiate sex, if she desires.

Endearing Statement

"Your eyes
are beautiful."

Quote

People need to be made more aware of the need to work at learning how to live because life is so quick and sometimes it goes away too quickly

Andy Warhol (1928–87), U.S. pop artist. Exhibition catalogue, Oct.-Nov. 1966, ICA, Boston.

SUGGESTION 13

Ask your lady to sit on your lap or next to you.

Put your arms around her. Hold her or make contact with her until she leaves your lap or your side.

Patience pays dividends.

Let her make the first move. Remember, if she kisses you, that may not mean she wants sex.

Endearing Statement

"Sometimes
in my mind,
I see you
standing on top
of a hill,
totally nude,
flying a kite."

Quote

To love, for us men, is to clasp one woman with our arms, feeling that she lives and breathes just as we do, suffers as we do, thinks with us, loves with us, and, above all, sins with us.

Baroness Orczy (1865–1947), Hungarian-born British novelist, playwright. Sir Percy Blakeney, in *I Will Repay,* ch. 7 (1906).

SUGGESTION 14

Using the pad of your ring finger, delicately, outline your lady's lips.

If she wears lip-gloss, put in on her lips, with a light touch.

Endearing Statement

"I like
the sounds
you make
when we
make love."

Quote

In love, there is always one who kisses and one who offers the cheek.

French Proverb. George Bernard Shaw adapted this proverb in *Heartbreak House,* act 2: "One turns the cheek: the other kisses it. One provides the cash: the other spends it."

SUGGESTION 15

While having dinner, hold your lady's hand.

Use your thumb to caress the outside of her fingers, thumb or hand, leaving the palm alone.

Look at her face until she asks, "What?"

Look a little longer, and with a slight squeeze of your hand, say, "You are lovely."

Endearing Statement

"You are
the most
beautiful woman
in the world to me."

Quote

If I were asked for a one line answer to the question "What makes a woman good in bed?" I would say, "A man who is good in bed."

Bob Guccione (b. 1930), U.S. publisher. Interview in Wendy Leigh, *Speaking Frankly* (1978).

SUGGESTION 16

Kiss your lady passionately for no reason.

Walk away. Return to her and kiss her gently.

If she begins to respond, be playful and tell her there is plenty more but that you are not easy.

Endearing Statement

"I am so glad
I choose you.
I am even happier
that you chose me."

Quote

Sex is one of the nine reasons for reincarnation. The other eight are unimportant.

Henry Miller (1891–1980), U.S. author. *Sexus,* ch. 21 (1949).

SUGGESTION 17

Gentlemen, this is big, big, big!

Be aware of timing. If she is in the middle of something, your chances of success are greatly diminished.

You may approach her and say, "I know you are busy but I would like a hug. Okay?"

Then, give her a 10-second hug.

Endearing Statement

"If I had it
to do all over,
I would live
each and every
moment with you again."

Quote

He who is in love is wise and is becoming wiser, sees newly every time he looks at the object beloved, drawing from it with his eyes and his mind those virtues which it possesses.

Ralph Waldo Emerson (1803–82), U.S. essayist, poet, philosopher. "The Method of Nature," oration, 11 Aug. 1841, delivered to the Society of the Adelphi, Waterville College, Me. (published in *The Works of Ralph Waldo Emerson,* 1889).

SUGGESTION 18

Ask your lady to go with you to buy sexy underwear that she would like to see you in.

Make sure you wear it.

Make sure she sees you putting in on in the morning to wear to work.

Better yet, before you go to bed, ask her to choose which sexy underwear she wants you to wear the next day. Let her savor thinking about you wearing your sexy thing just for her.

Endearing Statement

"I like the way
your eyes light up
when you play a joke on me."

Quote

Thy two breasts are like two young roes that are twins, which feed among the lilies.

Hebrew Bible. *Song of Solomon* 4:5.

SUGGESTION 19

Take your lady for a walk on the beach, around the block.

Ask her what her dreams are for her. Listen to her.

Think about this; this may be the only interactive adult talk she has had all day.

Endearing Statement

"I like
to see you
just after you
have stepped out
of the shower.
You are like
a morning flower
with dew on it."

Quote

Sex pleasure in woman...is a kind of magic spell; it demands complete abandon; if words or movements oppose the magic of caresses, the spell is broken.

Simone De Beauvoir (1908–86), French novelist, essayist. *The Second Sex,* bk. 2, pt. 4, ch. 3 (1953).

SUGGESTION 20

Before you leave in the morning, tell your lady you will be her love slave.

Ask her to think about what she wants. Make sure you do the things she wants, if reasonable to you.

Endearing Statement

"I like coming up to you
and nuzzling
my hair against you."

Quote

Stung by the splendour of a sudden thought.

Robert Browning (1812–89), English poet. *A Death in the Desert.*

SUGGESTION 21

After you make love, hold your lady in your arms for five minutes or more.

Hold her hand.

Caress her.

If you go to the bathroom, return to hold her.

This is important to most women.

Endearing Statement

"I like the softness
of your lips."

Quote

Familiar acts are beautiful through love.

Percy Bysshe Shelley (1792–1822), English poet. The Earth, in *Prometheus Unbound,* act 4.

SUGGESTION 22

Ask you lady if she would like to play the game of Cage and Capture and the Chase of the Merry Maiden.

Give her time to let her imagination play with scenes in her mind.

Endearing Statement

"You bring sunshine
into my life."

Quote

She's beautiful, and therefore to be wooed;
She is a woman, therefore to be won.

William Shakespeare (1564–1616), English dramatist,
poet. Suffolk, in *Henry VI Part 1,* act 5, sc. 5.

SUGGESTION 23

Let your lady know you find her beautiful when she steps from the shower with her hair all silky wet, or when she wakes with her soft, sleepy face, or when she is putting her nylons on with her leg hiked up on a chair, showcasing the curves of her leg.

Tell her that it excites you. Your lady does like to know and be told that she arouses you.

Endearing Statement

"When I think of you,
I want to sing.
Loud!"

Quote

Most men pursue pleasure with such breathless haste that they hurry past it.

Søren Kierkegaard (1813–55), Danish philosopher.
Either/Or, vol. 1, "Diapsalmata" (1843; tr. 1987).

SUGGESTION 24

Do something totally unexpected.

After your lady has taken a bite of ice cream, kiss her and use your tongue to get the ice cream.

Eat one strawberry or peach between the two of you without using hands.

Lick her nose.

Be playful.

Endearing Statement

"Thinking of you
makes me want
to pull a flower
from the neighbor's
yard and give it to you."

Quote

Passion, though a bad regulator, is a powerful spring.

Ralph Waldo Emerson (1803–82), U.S. essayist, poet, philosopher. The Conduct of Life, "Considerations by the Way" (1860).

SUGGESTION 25

Make love to your lady's hand while you are walking or talking.

Let your fingers and thumb softly glide over each finger, almost between the space of each finger. Leave the palm alone.

If sitting, take your thumb and forefinger and explore each of her fingers, horizontal, vertical and circling strokes.

Finish this by turning her palm upward. Kiss the palm and then kiss the pad of each finger.

Endearing Statement

"You have
great looking legs."

Quote

Skill makes love unending.

Ovid (43 B.C.-17 A.D.), Roman poet. *Ars Amatoria,* bk. 3.

SUGGESTION 26

Go to a hotel.

During strawberry season, dip a strawberry in wine or sparkling water and share.

Take a rose and dip it in the wine and trail it down your lady's throat, between her breasts.

Follow this with your tongue, licking her skin, tasting the mixture of her and the wine.

Suggesting an X rate movie may spoil the mood.

Endearing Statement

"You are my friend.
I am your friend."

Quote

Men have died from time to time, and worms have eaten them, but not for love.

William Shakespeare (1564–1616), English dramatist, poet. Rosalind, in *As You Like It,* act 4, sc. 1.

SUGGESTION 27

On the way to work the morning after you have made love, phone your lady.

Tell her, you love the taste of her and the delicate shade of color that washes over her body while making love.

Endearing Statement

"You are
my playmate."

Quote

A difference of tastes in jokes is a great strain on the affections.

George Eliot (1819–80), English novelist. *Daniel Deronda,* bk. 2, ch. 15 (1874–76).

SUGGESTION 28

Give her a 10-second hug.

I know I have repeated this; it is important for both of you.

Endearing Statement

"I like to see
you in red."

Quote

Sex is two plus two making five, rather than four. Sex is the X ingredient that you can't define, and it's that X ingredient between two people that make both a man and a woman good in bed. It's all relative. There are no rules.

Marty Feldman (1933–82), British comedian. Interview in Wendy Leigh, *Speaking Frankly* (1978).

SUGGESTION 29

Make a date with your lady to sit in front of the fireplace, on the patio, under a tree.

Make this free of children, animals, family, company and interruptions.

Turn the volume down on the answer machine to avoid the distraction of listening to who is calling.

Talk about dreams. In you mind, you can be and do anything. Go to that space and live your dreams.

Endearing Statement

"I like giving
you surprises."

Quote

Beauty is an ecstasy; it is as simple as hunger. There is really nothing to be said about it. It is like the perfume of a rose: you can smell it and that is all.

W. Somerset Maugham (1874–1965), British author. Ashenden, contesting the romanticization of beauty, in *Cakes and Ale,* ch. 11 (1930).

SUGGESTION 30

Call your lady at her work place.

Tell her, you were trying to imagine what she looks like, right now, if she were only in her lingerie.

Ask her what color panties she has on, or if she has any on.

Endearing Statement

"I like the way
your skin flushes
when we make love."

Quote

Sex is a conversation carried out by other means. If you get on well out of bed, half the problems of bed are solved.

Peter Ustinov (b. 1921), British actor, writer, director. Interview in Wendy Leigh, *Speaking Frankly* (1978).

SUGGESTION 31

Sing a love song to your lady.

Your voice does not have to be good. Put feelings into the words.

At the end of the song, hold her close.

Endearing Statement

"I like you.
I really like you!
I really like you a lot!!!"

Quote

A man has only one escape from his old self: to see a different self—in the mirror of some woman's eyes.

Clare Boothe Luce (1903–87), U.S. diplomat, writer. Mrs. Morehead, in *The Women,* act 1 (1936).

SUGGESTION 32

One day while out to dinner, breakfast, or coffee, tell you lady that it is taking all your effort to reframe from making love to her, right there in front of everyone.

Endearing Statement

"I like your smile."

Quote

Beauty seen is never lost,

God's colors all are fast.

John Greenleaf Whittier (1807–92), U.S. poet. *Sunset on the Bearcamp.*

SUGGESTION 33

Read to your lady.

Read a recipe from a cookbook. Caress the words with your mouth.

I suggest the dessert section.

Endearing Statement

"I like
when we walk,
hand in hand,
down the street."

Quote

Who has not felt the beauty of a woman's arm?—the unspeakable suggestions of tenderness that lie in the dimpled elbow, and all the varied gently-lessening curves, down to the delicate wrist, with its tiniest, almost imperceptible nicks in the firm softness.

George Eliot (1819–80), English novelist. *The Mill on the Floss,* bk. 6, ch. 10 (1860).

SUGGESTION 34

Go to church with your lady.

Put your arm around her when standing or when sitting.

Hold her hand.

Let her know you want God and everyone to know you find her desirable.

Endearing Statement

"I see
other men
watching you,
admiring you."

Quote

Lovers should also have their days off.

Natalie Clifford Barney (1876–1972), U.S.-born French author. Quoted in: George Wickes, *The Amazon of Letters,* ch. 10 (1976).

SUGGESTION 35

While at the movies, dinner, walking, anytime you are out, make a lot of physical contact.

Touch you lady.

Touch her arm.

Hold her hand.

Touch her cheek with the palm of your hand.

Give her a gentle kiss on the lips, or run your index finger down her cheek.

Gentlemen, just a note—women like you taking time with them.

Endearing Statement

"I like
when you link
your arm
in mine
when we walk."

Quote

To do the same thing over and over again is not only boredom: it is to be controlled by rather than to control what you do.

Heraclitus (c. 535 B.C.–c. 475 B.C.), Greek philosopher. *Herakleitos and Diogenes,* pt. 1, fragment 89 (tr. by Guy Davenport, 1976).

SUGGESTION 36

Give her a 10-second hug, a real good 10-second hug.

Endearing Statement

"I like
waking up
next to you
in the morning.
I like
going to sleep
with you at night."

Quote

The eyes those silent tongues of love.

Miguel de Cervantes (1547–1616), Spanish author.
Antonio's Amorous Complaint, in *Don Quixote,* pt. 1, bk.
2, ch. 3 (1605; tr. by P. Motteux).

SUGGESTION 37

Make your lady laugh.

Play. Set aside a time each day for fun.

Laugh.

You may even want to tickle her, skip stones with her or walk the railroad tracks with her.

Endearing Statement

"I love you
more every day."

Quote

God gives every bird his worm, but He does not throw it into the nest.

P. D. James (b. 1920), British mystery writer. Jonah the tramp, in *Devices and Desires,* ch. 40 (1989), quoting a wayside pulpit.

SUGGESTION 38

Come up behind your lady and put your arm around her, resting it on her chest bone.

Lift her hair, then kiss the nape of her neck.

Kiss slowly. Tickle her neck with the tip of your tongue.

Blow gently. Kiss her again, gently.

Turn her around and kiss her neck. If she offers her mouth, kiss her lips.

Endearing Statement

"You are
sweetness
in my life."

Quote

Love gives naught but itself and takes naught butfrom itself.

Love possesses not nor would it be possessed;
For love is sufficient unto love.

Kahlil Gibran (1883–1931), Lebanese poet, novelist. *The Prophet* (1923).

SUGGESTION 39

Talk with your lady. Talk with her about anything under the sun, except problems.

Ask her questions. Let her know you hear her.

All the time you are doing this, touch her arm or hold her hand.

Gentlemen, this is important! Stimulate the brain and all else follows.

Endearing Statement

"I like
waking up in the night
knowing that you are there."

Quote

Imagination is the voice of daring. If there is anything Godlike about God it is that. He dared to imagine everything.

Henry Miller (1891–1980), U.S. author. *Sexus*, ch. 14 (1949).

SUGGESTION 40

Ask your lady to have breakfast or lunch with you.

Ask her to spend some time at your office because you like looking at her face.

Endearing Statement

"There are times
I feel
so much love
for you
that I
would be willing
to climb
the tallest ladder
to bring you a star."

Quote

Pleasant words are as an honeycomb, sweet to the soul, and health to the bones.

Hebrew Bible. *Proverbs* 16:24.

SUGGESTION 41

Hold hands.

Hold hands.

Hold hands.

Make contact.

Make contact.

Make contact.

Endearing Statement

"I like
when you smile
into flowers."

Quote

Nothing great was ever achieved without enthusiasm.

Ralph Waldo Emerson (1803–82), U.S. essayist, poet, philosopher. *Essays,* "Circles" (First Series, 1841).

SUGGESTION 42

Send your lady a mushy, love card for absolutely no reason other than you want her to know you "like" and "love" her.

Better yet, make her a love card.

Endearing Statement

"When you
are away,
I feel
an empty space
which can
only be filled
by you."

Quote

Men greet each other with a sock on the arm, women with a hug, and the hug wears better in the long run.

Edward Hoagland (b. 1932), U.S. novelist, essayist. "Heaven and Nature," in *Harper's* (March 1988; repr. in *Heart's Desire,* 1988).

SUGGESTION 43

Tell your lady you will be her "boy toy" that evening.

She will be the Mistress and have her way with you.

Endearing Statement

"I love to watch
you dress
in the morning,
especially
when you
dress slowly."

Quote

Imagination is the eye of the soul.

Joseph Joubert (1754–1824), French essayist, moralist. *Pensées,* no. 42 (1842).

SUGGESTION 44

Once a week, while nude, or almost nude, hold your lady and caress her body without making love to her.

Hold her for however long she wants.

If she initiates love making, go ahead. Make sure the signals are very clear. Learn her signals.

Endearing Statement

"With you,
my dance card
is filled."

Quote

Jupiter, not wanting man's life to be wholly gloomy and grim, has bestowed far more passion than reason—you could reckon the ration as twenty-four to one. Moreover, he confined reason to a cramped corner of the head and left all the rest of the body to the passions.

Desiderius Erasmus (c. 1466–1536), Dutch humanist. *Praise of Folly,* ch. 16 (1509).

SUGGESTION 45

Tell your lady you want to wash her hair. Do so.

Tell her you want to paint her toenails. Do so.

Give her toes a real good massage.

Endearing Statement

"You are very pretty."

Quote

Love is a great beautifier.

Louisa May Alcott (1832–88), U.S. author. *Little Women,* pt. 2, ch. 1 (1869).

SUGGESTION 46

Bring your lady a single flower for no reason.

Caress her face with it; watch her face light up with surprise.

Endearing Statement

"I like
the way you move."

Quote

For what is love itself, for the one we love best?—an enfolding of immeasurable cares which yet are better than any joys outside our love.

George Eliot (1819–80), English novelist, editor. *Daniel Deronda,* bk. 8, ch. 69 (1876).

SUGGESTION 47

Towel your lady dry after a shower or bath.

It is a gentle patting dry, as if she were a precious art object that you do not want damaged.

Dry her everywhere. Some places, like the ears, can be finished of with a blow dry.

Endearing Statement

"I love you
dearly."

Quote

Friendship is Love without his wings!

Lord Byron (1788–1824), English poet. *L'Amitié est L'Amour Sans Ailes.*

SUGGESTION 48

Kiss your lady.

Kiss her face.

Kiss her eyes.

Kiss her nose.

Kiss her chin.

Kiss her upper lip.

Kiss her lower lip.

Kiss her cheeks.

Kiss her neck.

Kiss her ears.

Kiss her hair.

Let her know you like her eyes, her nose, her chin, her lips, her cheeks, her neck, her ears, her hair.

Gentlemen, leave the hickeys to the teenagers.

Endearing Statement

"I look
forward to telling
you how much I care."

Quote

When all is said and done, friendship is the only trustworthy fabric of the affections. So-called love is a delirious inhuman state of mind: when hot it substitutes indulgence for fair play; when cold it is cruel, but friendship is warmth in cold, firm ground in a bog.

Miles Franklin (1879–1954), Australian authoress. *My Career Goes Bung,* ch. 19 (written 1900; published 1946).

SUGGESTION 49

Read to your lady from the novel or magazine she is reading.

The sound of your voice can be very arousing.

Endearing Statement

"Let me
hold you
gently
in my arms."

Quote

The greatest sweetener of human life is Friendship. To raise this to the highest pitch of enjoyment, is a secret which but few discover.

Joseph Addison (1672–1719), English essayist.
Interesting Anecdotes, Memoirs, Allegories, Essays, and Poetical Fragments, "Of Friendship" (1794).

SUGGESTION 50

Do the 10-second hug.

A woman enjoys the feel of her man's body in embrace.

Endearing Statement

"You are tops."

TRICK TO THE TRADE #1

Timing is everything.

The time to start is right now. If you want to make love in the evening, start in the morning.

Approaching your lady five minutes before you want sex to begin foreplay will usually be ineffectual.

TRICK TO THE TRADE #2

The temperature of the surroundings needs to be conducive for your lady to respond to you.

If you like to see her in shorts and a skimpy blouse, then adjust the thermostat to her liking.

You might try taking off your shirt and showing her some skin.

It is important to do this some time before you initiate anything.

Give generously of attentive details.

TRICK TO THE TRADE #3

Fantasies can be fun.

Some women will play them out and others will not.

If you pressure her to perform any fantasies, yours or hers, then, you may never hear another fantasy verbalized, much less experienced.

TRICK TO THE TRADE #4

Give generously in allowing her time.

Keep trying.

A *tried it once and it did not work* attitude decreases the passion in the relationship with your lady.

TRICK TO THE TRADE #5

Create mystery and drama to heighten
the pleasure for you and your lady.

PASSION FORMULA

Desire +

Commitment +

Action =

Reward